MADE TO MAKE IT

Shushan-Eduth: A life full of Testimonies

Abisola Akinola-Babatunde

MADE TO MAKE IT

Author's Contact:
abisolababs21@gmail.com

Commendations

Know yourself. It is the most important thing you can do. Self-awareness is central to leadership, and this book undoubtedly delivers this message. Self-awareness is a trait—a practice—that each of us can always improve. Due to Abisola's extensive experience in the academic and professional terrain, MADE TO MAKE IT encourages and inspires everyone to be their most authentic self and live a fulfilling life. This is definitely a must read!

Grant A. Erhuanga (Ph.D.), USA
Founder & CEO of Innovazing
Founder & CEO, Mavasive Leadership Institute
Certified Leadership Coach
Project Management Professional & Six Sigma Trained

This is a remarkable and timely book by a true spiritual friend. MADE TO MAKE IT is certain to bring out the best in everyone and serve as an inspiration for anyone in a challenging phase of their lives.

Abayomi Alayande (Ph.D.), South Korea
Researcher, Gwangju Institute of Science & Technology

I love MADE TO MAKE IT. Life does not give to any man what he or she deserves but demands. The author has tenaciously brought to fore the missing link between the champions and the mediocre. I will like to sound a note of warning to every intending reader of this failure antidote, if you're not ready for a new level, a shift from the usual, a flight from the box, mental muscle for exploits, don't touch this book. But if you're, holding this book is a moment of significance, opening the first chapter is a journey to greatness and closing the last chapter is a LIFE FULL OF TESTIMONIES. I congratulate you for having a copy, reading it and applying the nuggets.

Seyon-Lanre D. Jonah (MBA, Ph.D.), Nigeria
Director of Education-For-All-Initiative
& Advocate for OpenData, Education & Research

At the core of any successful life is self-understanding. MADE TO MAKE IT, a book birthed out of practical experiences, emphasizes this. Abisola Akinola-Babatunde, a purpose-driven lady, has put together in this book vital life changing principles. Read, learn and apply the life propelling nuggets she shares in the book.

Ajala Adewole (Ph.D.), China
Researcher at University of Chinese Academy of
Sciences

Abisola Akinola-Babatunde is a selfless woman who is passionate about the physical, psychological and spiritual growth of young people. This book, MADE TO MAKE IT, has the potentials to transform your life. It is a confidence booster. It will help you know who you truly are, what you have the ability to become, then show you how you can become it.

Otome Justin Dafevwakpo, Nigeria
Pastor, Public Speaker, Award-winning Leader
Recipient of the Honorary Lifetime Membership of
PATRAL
Founder of Pearl Educational Consult

In MADE TO MAKE IT, Abisola Akinola-Babatunde, whom I have known to be passionate about purpose, challenges her readers that to be relevant, significant and successful in their life pursuit, they must be willing to face stumbling blocks embrace their mistakes, take advantage of waiting periods and ultimately trust God at every stage of life.

Busola Adun, UK
Founder, The Noble Woman Ministry

Dedication

To my awe-inspiring husband, Akinola, and my honorable son, Dexstar; and to everyone who is determined to make it irrespective of what life throws at them.

Table Of Contents

Acknowledgement

All thanks to God who keeps setting me up to make it; to Him be all the glory for His matchless love, favor, mercy and grace.

Special thanks to my dear husband who has been a major source of inspiration in achieving my dreams. I also appreciate your efforts and work on this book as my chief editor. Sincere gratitude to my gracious son for being considerate during the process of writing this book.

I must say thank you to my parents, Barr. and Mrs. Oguntoye, for their sacrifices and help in laying good foundation for my greatness.

I deeply appreciate all the people who took time to write commendations for the book. My profound gratitude to Femi Adun for writing the foreword.

I am grateful to my family, friends, and everyone who contributed to my life and helped me to become a better person.

Metaphorically, quantum leap could mean giant strides, above average, possibilities, exponential growth, increase, or uncommon success rate. When it comes to living or experiencing quantum dimensions; you must be ready to take a leap. Your leap of faith is the requirement for quantum dimensions.

Every human being is intrinsically wired and designed in such a magnificent way to succeed in the most outstanding way. You are born to be great. You are **made to make it.** However, it has been said over and over that the journey of a thousand miles begins with a step, which means to experience a quantum leap in any area of life, you must begin with a leap of faith. Proverbially, your five loaves and two fish can feed 5000, if only you dare to share.

History is full of men and women who made it in various spheres and proven this book not only true but relevant by every standard. The challenge I see with the other parties who feel success is an exclusive right of a few is the failure to understand that success is not a respecter of people either by color or race; success answers to principles, character and God. However, it has become a familiar phrase to hear many Christians say, "they are waiting on God", whilst there is nothing wrong in waiting on God but waiting on God could result into a lack of progress if waiting doesn't lead to taking actions that are based on faith in Him and guided by His wisdom. If there is a book in the entire bible that contains several people taking giant strides, walking in impossible realms all at the same time is the book of Acts and this is because of ordinary people acting in faith; they took a leap of faith. You can make it, excel greatly and walk in unlimited possibilities if you dare to act contrary to the prevalent circumstances of your life.

God's word is clear that prayer without an act of faith will not change the situation that looks daunting and impossible. It wouldn't matter how many times a week Jesus showed up in Peter's boat; nothing would have changed if Peter had not acted on what Jesus told him to do – he wouldn't have made it. In most cases it's not us waiting on the God; it's God waiting on us!

Effectual faith is not factual; it is actual. Factual faith not translated into actual faith will lead to lack of progress. Those that will work in unlimited possibilities are those that have mastered taking steps of faith, acting in obedience to the possibilities they have conceived in their heart. Don't spend so much time musing over your predicament and miss out on taking ownership of the action that will change your situation.

Be clear on what you want to achieve. Clarity makes acting in faith easier. Before action can be the ultimate response to an inspiration, divine revelation or instruction clarity must be established. Uncertainty most times is what leads to hesitation. It is unlikely not to act when there is clarity, especially when it provides the means for positive change in one's life.

I am delighted that author, Abisola Babatunde has decided to release such a timely book with timeless truths to inspire and guide not just her readers but an entire present generation to believe that everyone is born with the potential to make it. She has also provided practical guidance to aid readers to achieve success in their pursuit of personal development and progress. I have always admired Mrs. Abisola's keenness to excellence which again is visible in this project for which I must commend her as well as recommend this book to anyone seeking to make a paradigm shift from their current position. Thank you for pouring your heart into each page of this book. I pray that your effort will impact on the decisions of many across the globe in Jesus name, Amen! Well done!

Apostle Femi Adun
President, Eagle World Outreach

Introduction

In life, only people who don't have plans to move forward will most probably have a stress free journey. This is primarily because they would just be on a particular spot. They wouldn't have to face stumbling blocks, road bumps, traffic, turning and so on.

Anyone who plans to go far would have to be prepared for challenges. The journey to success, the road that leads to the desired destination is not without some or many rough patches. It is not always smooth. "A smooth sea never made a skilled mariner". Success in life's journey is full of adventure and it is not for weaklings, it's meant for victors. As humans, running away from our mistakes is a mistake in itself.

MADE TO MAKE IT teaches the importance of understanding yourself and bringing out the best in you. It's a reminder that life is a precious gift and God has provided everything needed to live life to the fullest. It talks about the need to selflessly care and love people and shows the importance of a forgiving heart. In the book, you will find that you can't afford to compromise your stand and integrity for God no matter what. This book emphasizes the need to maximize waiting time and understand divine timing. In all, we need God; His divine help is inevitable. I also shared my personal testimonies which I believe will inspire you.

This masterpiece is an encouragement not to quit. Sometimes, all that is needed is taking one more step, giving it one more try, and push further just a little more, for the desired life to fully manifest. Life is not void of challenges, so we have to fight to overcome the storms and tough times. There is a popular acronym known as WYSIWYG which means what you see is what you get. But my own definition of WYSIWYG and my advice to you is to "Whet Your Stance, It is Worth Your Generosity".

This book is specifically designed to coach you through directions and teachings from God, men and life experiences. It's filled with hope for everyone who is going through or will possibly go through difficult times at one point or the other. I am fully convinced that it will propel you to see the need to stand up, challenge your challenges and go the extra mile which is usually never crowded. It's a push to live the life you are made for. You are MADE TO

MAKE IT; you are made to have a LIFE FULL OF TESTIMONIES.

Toast to a LIFE FULL OF TESTIMONIES (SHUSHAN-EDUTH)!

SELF: THE FIRST GIANT TO OVERCOME

Knowing God will help you discover yourself. He formed you based on what he knew, sanctified and ordained you for.

Change your self-image, don't focus on yourself; focus on God. It is in God that you can find yourself.

God did not make you to be average. He has deposited great things in you. It's your responsibility to discover and dart in the direction!

Many times, the steps you are afraid to take always connect you to the ones you are looking forward to.

1

SELF: THE FIRST GIANT TO OVERCOME

Someone once shared a story of an old Cherokee. The old Cherokee told his grandson, "My son, there is a battle between two wolves inside us all. One is evil; it is anger, jealousy, greed, resentment, inferiority, lies, and ego. The other is good; it is joy, peace, love, hope, humility, kindness, empathy and truth. The boy thought about it and asked, "Grandfather, which wolf wins?" The old man quietly replied, "The one you feed".

Self is the type of person you are, it is your character and your typical behavior. Self is said to be your greatest enemy but it can also be your friend. It helps in making choices due to its contradictory nature to the spirit. It helps you to be determined and focused. Indeed, self is said to be your greatest enemy but you can make it your friend. You have to deal with yourself before dealing with any other giants. Once you believe it can be done, you can achieve it. You can become a better YOU. Discover your identity; who do you think you are? Joel Osteen said, "You will never rise above the image you have of yourself in your own mind".

Jeremiah 1:5 (KJV) affirms, "Before I formed thee, I knew thee…I sanctified thee and I ordained thee". To launch into your ministry or fulfill purpose, knowing God and understanding yourself is very important. Knowing God will help you discover yourself. God formed you based on what he knew, sanctified and ordained you for. You don't value what you don't know. You need to be sanctified or set apart. This means working on and training yourself. You can't be everywhere or be close friends with everybody around and expect to live a purposeful life-a life you have been ordained for. Pastor Nike Adeyemi says, "You need to be comfortable in your own company".

Change your self-image. While trying to understand yourself, the focus should not be on you, it should be on God. It is in God that you can find your true identity. Celebrate your discovery and become what you believe. To receive, we have to believe. What you believe has much greater impact in your life than what others believe. Believe in yourself! Develop a prosperous mindset. God did not design you to be average. He has deposited great things in you. It's your responsibility to discover and dart in that direction! The step you are afraid to take is always connected to the ones you are looking forward to.

Furthermore, be happy with who you are, be the best you can be. Have a good self-esteem and always appreciate yourself. Remember, no one is in charge of your happiness except you.

2

YOU HAVE A
LIFE TO LIVE

You can't afford to fail people who believe in you, you can't afford to fail people who look up to you, you can't afford to fail yourself and most importantly you can't afford to fail God.

Life is a precious gift given to us by the most precious one, and a special present presented by the most special one, so cherish it.

The creator has made you in his image, giving you a blank check to achieve all you can; you don't have limits because God has no limits.

Time is one of the greatest things we can sacrifice because it can't be bought or redeemed. There is no blessing without lesson. The most demanding things in life are things that add value, things that are right, things that lead to success.

Things don't get easier; we are the ones to get better and stronger.

The devil does not mind you speaking words of faith as long as you don't take steps of faith.

If you believe you have to live a caring life, then don't just believe or talk about it, care indeed. If you believe in godliness don't just say it, live it.

2

YOU HAVE A
LIFE TO LIVE

You have a life to live, you have dreams to transform to reality, and you have a purpose to fulfill. There are people looking up to you; you can't afford to fail them, you can't afford to fail yourself and most importantly you can't afford to fail God. You have a responsibility to triumph and conquer all the obstacles that can stop you from living a life of fulfillment.

Life is a precious gift given to us by the most precious one, and a special present presented by the most special one, so cherish it. God made you a victor and gave you great potentials, it's up to you to fully utilize and maximize those potentials. The creator has made you in his image, giving you a blank check to achieve all you can. You don't have limits because God has no limits. The ball is in your court. God has given you the power to your will. It's now your decision to make what you want out of it. You either make a right choice or a wrong one. It is written in the scriptures that God has set before you life and death, blessing and cursing, and he advised you to choose life, that you may live. There are several things to consider when deciding the kind of life we want to live. Some of them are discussed here:

Live a sacrificial and disciplined life: For everything that has value, there is a need for sacrifice. Do you feel that you are sacrificing too much? Don't worry, it will soon make sense. Your sacrifice can't be too much. Even the salvation that Christians proclaim is free had to be heavily paid for by Jesus before we could access it. And, for us to keep enjoying the salvation, we need to keep sacrificing daily, overcoming our flesh in order to live right. To have a life full of testimonies, sacrifice is very important. You need to be ready to invest time; it is one of the greatest sacrifices we can make because it can't be bought or redeemed. We should also be willing to sacrifice energy and money too. There is no blessing without lesson. The most demanding things in life are things that add value, things that are right, things that lead to success. For example in your academics, you have to study and pass your exams to move to the next level. To excel financially you need to be disciplined and buy fewer liabilities in other to acquire assets. To succeed in your career you must be committed and be ready to make sacrifices. A successful and beautiful marriage requires tireless and creative efforts. Things don't get easier; we are the ones that must get better and stronger.

Set priorities right: Give your energy to what matters. Don't use your strength and energy on things or activities that don't matter. This affords you enough time for the things that are important. Check your life, who are the people you attract? You always attract like-minded people. If you feel unserious people come to you, check your life to see if you exhibit some levels of unseriousness. How do you look? How do you behave? How do you do things?

Take actions: The devil does not mind you speaking words of faith as long as you don't take steps of faith. People most times talk about the second chapter of James in the bible and refer to 'faith without work' as just having faith and not working or having a job. James was talking about what I call "the deeds of faith"; he was referring to action towards what you claim you believe in. If you believe you have to live a caring life, then don't just believe or talk about it, care indeed. If you believe in godliness don't just say it, live life in such a way that people will see you and say you are truly godly, not just because they hear you say it but because they see you live it. Follow what you believe in and give your all to it. James went on in verse 19 of the same chapter, "You believe that there is one God. Good! Even the demons believe that—and shudder" (NIV). What makes the difference is not just believing in something or someone, but taking the corresponding action about what you believe.

Life is that great event you don't just walk into. It's an event you get prepared and dressed for! There is no excuse, we can't afford to fail. Life is a precious gift, cherish it! It is appointed unto men once to die, but after this death comes judgment. You have only one life. Live it graciously!

THE HEART OF COMPASSION: A KEY TO SELFLESSNESS

No one can claim to truly know God and continue to live in hatred or dislike.

Making the world a better place makes people stronger in other to easily overcome temptations. Let's uphold each other.

If you can't show love, don't show hatred. Just let people be, don't make things worse for them if you can't make it better.

No one can find true and satisfying happiness in trying to make others sad.

Keep the heart of compassion open, this world is desperate to experience the love and compassion of God already deposited in you, His child.

We can't love ourselves the right way if we don't love God. And, surely, it is difficult to love others if we don't love God.

Loving God is the root of living in love. How can we love imperfect being when we can't love the perfect Being?

3

THE HEART OF COMPASSION: A KEY TO SELFLESSNESS

No man is an island. We all need people in our journey through life. To get people to stand and help us in difficult times we have to be caring and loving. What's your attitude to the people around you? How do you treat strangers and the less privileged? What goes around comes around. Life is full of ups and downs. Washington Carver once said, "How far you go in life depends on your being tender with the young, compassionate with the striving and tolerant of the weak and strong. Someday in life you will have been all of these".

Walk and work with people. You can't do everything on your own. Acts 6:2 says, "Then the twelve summoned the multitude of the disciples and said, "It is not desirable that we should leave the word of God and serve tables." This is a practical example of leadership and delegation. You can't be the one to give the word and serve the table at the same time.

Don't judge others. Judging people is a sign of pride. No one is perfect and anyone can make mistakes. It's unfortunate that we have classified sins and errors in such a way that we feel our mistakes are not as grave as others' mistakes. Sin is sin whether light or heavy. We can't say we truly know God and live in hatred, dislike or judge others. When I was much younger I found myself judging my mates, ladies I felt were not living right. As I grew up, I discovered I was just privileged to know the things I knew and grace kept me. I celebrated this as a spiritual growth and I made deliberate efforts to stop judging others.

Let's live with others with love and not fear. This makes it easy for us to fight temptations. Yes, temptations will come but what we do and equip ourselves with help us overcome temptations. We should feed our spirit. Let's take a look at a scenario: there is a very delicious but forbidden meal. We have two men of character (note: highly disciplined men) they saw the food but are not allowed to eat it. One is hungry and the other is not. Both can refuse to yield to the temptation of eating the meal but it is easier for the satisfied man to resist than the man who is hungry. Let's make the world a better place, a place that makes people stronger so they can easily overcome temptations. We should uphold one another.

When Abraham's servant saw Rebekah and asked for water, Rebekah even said I will give your camels too. This shows that Rebekah had great attributes and good character. She did not insult Eliezer or insist that he gets the water himself. Rebekah's attitude helped her connect with greatness. If you can't show love, don't show hatred. Just let people be, don't make things worse for them if you can't make them better. There is no true happiness in trying to make others sad.

We cannot reap what we have not sown. Show love to people around you, it pays. There is a saying that, "when dealing with yourself use your head, but when dealing with others use your heart". It's unfortunate that most times we do the opposite. Humans have the tendency to be naturally selfish. Keep the heart of compassion open, this world is desperate to experience the love and compassion of God which He has deposited in us, His children. I love this quote by Carson McCullers, "The closest thing to being cared for is to care for someone else". Pastor Nike Adeyemi said "be known for kindness and positivity. We all know that we need it to support one another".

In order to love others, we have to love God. I know there is a popular statement that, we can't love others if we don't love ourselves. Here is the trick; we can't love ourselves the right way if we don't love God. And, surely, it is difficult to love others if we don't love God. The scripture says "Love your neighbor as yourself", not after yourself, and this is not easy, we can only be able to do this if we follow the first and greatest commandment which is to love God with all our heart, with all our soul, and with our entire mind. Loving God is the root of living in love. How can we love imperfect being when we can't love the perfect Being? When we love God, we care about what He feels and what He wants. This helps us to have the nature of God and overcome the selfish desires of the flesh, for God is love.

4

THE BEAUTY OF A FORGIVING HEART

You don't have to forgive people because they deserve it or requested for it, you forgive because you deserve peace and God deserves your obedience.

There is no hurt, no disappointment, and no offence that is unforgivable.

Two sets of people you must forgive; everybody and yourself. It

*is difficult for you to move on if you don't forgive yourself.
Forgiveness leads to freedom.*

*As long as you deserve peace and God's forgiveness
then everyone deserves your forgiveness.*

*The people who disappoint you or fail you may not have had the
intention; that shows the limitations of man.*

*The fact that you regretted your actions doesn't mean you repented.
Regret is not the same as repentance. Running away from your mistake
is a mistake.*

*There's a need to shed weight so you can fight to finish, the journey is too
far than to weigh yourself down with loads of unforgiveness.*

Make peace with your past so it won't affect the present and future.

4
THE BEAUTY OF A FORGIVING HEART

Ward Beecher said and I quote, "Forgiveness ought to be like a canceled note, torn in two and burned up, so that it can never be shown against the man who offended us".

To forgive means to grant a pardon. Relationships are inevitable. There's a need to keep in mind that the people we deal with are human. Due to human limitations, they have a high tendency to hurt, disappoint and offend other humans. We need to be prepared to forgive always. A step higher is to forgive people even before they hurt us. That's a great sign of maturity. We don't forgive people because they deserve it or they requested for it, we forgive because we deserve peace and God deserves our obedience. To live a life full of testimonies we need God. Unforgiveness will hinder our free access to the Creator. So, when you know you can't do it alone without God, why not forgive and move on. True forgiveness does not come easy. It takes conscious effort. There is no hurt, no disappointment, and no offence that is unforgivable. There are two sets of people we must forgive in life:

First, **Everybody:** It is a command from God to forgive. As long as you deserve peace and God's forgiveness then everyone deserves your forgiveness no matter what. Letting go of offences means your trust is not in man. In John 2:23-24, Jesus did not commit to those who even believe in Him, because he knew man and knows man will always be man. The people who disappoint us or fail us may not have had the intentions to do so, that shows the limitations of man.

Don't hold on to offence; let's learn from the great Teacher, Jesus. In John 13:10-11, "Jesus told him, whoever has already bathed needs only to wash his feet, and he will be completely clean. And you are clean, though not all of you." For He knew who would betray Him, that is why He said, "Not all of you are clean." Jesus ate with Judas till the very end and washed his feet knowing he would betray Him and had given himself to the devil. He still cared for Judas.

In addition to forgiving everybody, the second person that needs your forgiveness is you. You must forgive **Yourself!** You are human, you are not perfect, you make mistakes, you take wrong decisions in life and this can cause you not to forgive yourself. It is difficult for you to move on if you don't forgive yourself. Unforgiveness can lead to self-pity and depression. Forgiveness leads to freedom. Stop blaming yourself. Don't ever think you have done so much harm that God can't forgive you. That's a lie! No sin is unforgivable once you repent. Kindly note, there is a difference between true repentance and regret. The fact that you regretted your actions doesn't mean you repented. Regret is not the same as repentance. It is left for you to accept responsibility and move on. Remember "Running away from your mistake is a mistake".

Nothing should bring you low to the point of hatred and unforgiveness. Anything that controls your emotion has authority over you. Be careful. Free yourself from such weight. There's a need to shed those weight so you can fight to finish. The journey is too far to weigh yourself down with loads of unforgiveness. Make peace with your past so it won't affect the present and future!

5

DO NOT COMPROMISE

In your journey in life, you'll have to choose from different options, stand right! No matter how easy compromising looks like, do not yield to it.

It is not everything that looks or sounds good that is inspired by God.

Stop lowering God's standard to fit in the world's standard all in the name of civilization and modernization.

Sometimes in life we don't know when the reward of living right and not compromising will come, it might not be immediate but it will surely come.

To stay under God's roof you have to follow His rule.

Know God and remain in him. Start and stay!

For you to birth some kinds of solutions or miracles there is a standard, tap into grace to live God's standard and do not settle for less.

Don't take grace for granted.

Integrity and honesty are like information saved in a memory card that can never corrupt, they last forever.

5

DO NOT COMPROMISE

The word compromise can be defined in different ways but in this context, it is an endangering of reputation. For example: a compromise of one's integrity. It can also mean to allow your principles to be less strong, or your standards or morals to be lower. It also means to expose oneself to suspicion, discredit or mischief. In your journey in life, you'll have to choose from different options. I encourage you to stand right. No matter how easy compromising looks like, do not yield to it. Can't forget a popular adage that says, "Whatever you compromise to get you'll compromise to keep". Nothing is hidden forever! Doing the right thing can be difficult but in the long run, it pays. Gilbert K. Chesterton said, "To have a right to do a thing is not at all the same as to be right doing it". What you compromise to get will not last. Compromise leads to regret. It reduces your worth and shows your lack or loss of integrity. A teacher once told me, "The best of life does not come easily, the most admired things do not come cheap, and the best character did not take a day to be built". For every prize, there is a price to pay. Don't settle for less!

Don't find excuse for compromise, sometimes we hide under the covering of trying to show love to or care for people doing the wrong things in order to change them. When confronted, we say things like, "If you want to catch a monkey, act like a monkey". In trying to convert unbelievers we shouldn't compromise God's standard. Yes, it is good to show love but don't be equally yoked. You can't have a changed mind and no change in outward actions. We are to take our stand and show others how to do the right thing without using it as the excuse to do the wrong things.

The world is thirsty for undiluted truth. Our primary assignment as Christians is to spread the gospel. We may use different methods but in the end, it should glorify Jesus. Like Jesus while he was on earth, he won some souls by healing, some by eating with them, others by preaching to them immediately or performing miracles. But all in all, his actions glorified God.

Psalm 82:6, says, "I said, You are gods, And all of you are children of the Most High". Most times we see this verse just in the light of the power and authority we have in Christ, or our right to success, prosperity and promises of God. We go for the authority to command, loose and bind neglecting the fact that this also portrays the fact that we are meant to have God's attribute. These attributes include holiness. We should be holy like our God and represent him in total, not just in some areas we feel comfortable with.

Don't get it mixed up. The possessed damsel discussed in Acts 16:16-18 was saying the correct thing but with the wrong spirit. She said the truth about the apostles but that didn't get to their head to make them compromise. It is not everything that looks or sounds good that is inspired by God.

It is so pathetic that we live in a world where evil is celebrated and painted as good. Today, many lower God's standard to fit into the world's standard all in the name of civilization and modernization. We have seen several situations even in the movie industry. Some movies try to portray that someone who compromised got to the top while someone else who did not compromise good standard ended up as a cleaner or with any other petty job, without making it clear that you can compromise to get to the top but you can't compromise to remain at the top. It might take time but the time will reveal the truth. I remember when I was in a private college preparing for the university; I sat for an examination called GCE in my country, Nigeria. GCE is like an A-levels exam and I took the exam in SSS2, a class before my college final year. I did not take the examinations in my school because we were meant to take it in SSS3 but I got permission from the school and registered online. I was given one of the centers which happened to be a public school. Some students naturally dread mathematics. On the day we were meant to write our mathematics exam, many were afraid including me. The exam turned out to be very tough because I was in SSS 2, I prepared for the exam myself, and we were not yet taught some of the topics at school. Almost all of us who wrote the exam found it difficult. So people opted for examination malpractice. In one class I heard they wrote answers on the board and I was really glad I was not in that class. In my own class they passed answers on paper, and some of our invigilators and supervisors were aware. Though I didn't know this work and I was so scared of failure, I refused to take the paper. I just put my trust in God and did what I could do. I got a pass (E) in the course. That was below the average pass mark which was credit (C) at the time. I felt bad. But that didn't stop my admission to the university, God changed the rule for my sake, instead of the criteria for Arts students to have credit in mathematics, it was changed to anything higher than fail (F). There were people who got higher grades but did not gain admission. Sometimes in life, we don't know when the reward of living right, standing for integrity and not compromising will come. It might not be immediate but it will surely come.

In Luke 4:5-7 (NIV), "The devil led Jesus up to a high place and showed Him in an instant all the kingdoms of the world. And he said to Him, "I will give you all their authority and splendor; it has been given to me, and I can give it to anyone I want to. If you worship me, it will all be yours." Imagine the devil trying to deceive Jesus to fall for him with what Jesus has power over and owns already. The whole world that has been and will be under the control of Jesus is what the devil used to tempt Him. Isn't that funny? This is what the devil does even now to believers, trying to lure believers to get things the wrong way, things we can possess in Christ Jesus. We experience delay, trials and challenges to help us get better and grow spiritually. Some of us will not regard God again if things are always rosy. Even when things are not that easy, it is difficult to have quality time with God because the world system is designed to make us forget God.

In Luke 4:13, it was recorded the devil departed from Jesus for a season. That means the devil will not stop tempting us, he can only go for a season and that is why it is important to constantly be on the guard, never relent. To stay under God's roof you have to follow His rule. Live the word of God. Know God and remain in him. Start and stay!

In Jesus' genealogy, yes there were prostitutes, adulterers but it was a virgin that gave birth to Jesus, the Messiah. For you to birth some kinds of solutions or miracles there is a standard, tap into grace to live God's standard do not settle for less.

Beware of compromising relationships. The easiest way to overcome such relationships is to prevent them from the beginning. Be careful in opening your heart. Love is strong and we need to be careful whom we open our heart to.

Guard your heart as much as possible, because when you are in love it is difficult to think without being sentimental. That is why sometimes you just wonder why that lady can't leave the guy or vice versa despite the warning signs and glaring issues. The best thing is not to start things on the wrong foundation. It is much easier to guard your heart to prevent such occurrences than to get involved, and try to get back up.

Don't take grace for granted. We should not do things out of fear, but at the same time we should not take things for granted. We lock the door of the house not because we have faith only on the door to keep us safe but we won't be careless to just leave it open. Let's leave our lives in confidence and in such a way that we don't joke with it, God should not be tested, yes we know God will protect us but we shouldn't test him or take grace for granted.

Integrity and honesty are like information saved in a memory card that can never corrupt, they last forever. The reward of not compromising is not only immediate but generational. Your children will even enjoy it and thank you for it. There is pride, blessing and lesson in it.

6

YOU HAVE WHAT IT TAKES

In life there are no class mates, everyone is in his or her own class. No same set or same level, we all operate on different levels and timing.

The right direction will lead to the great destination.

Celebrate your strength instead of capitalizing on your weakness.

People will misunderstand you and make you feel worse but don't lose yourself.

Take to corrections but don't lose who you are in trying to adjust to peoples' measures.

Everybody can not like or accept you no matter how hard you try, even Jesus who is perfect and with no sins and blemish was hated and rejected.

Success is the best avenge for your haters. Go and succeed!

YOU HAVE
WHAT IT TAKES

You were created to solve one or some of the problems in the world. You either reduce the problems or add to the problems. You are a conqueror, you are a victor, and you are an achiever. There is a king in you. You have what it takes to triumph. You have the ability to face the giants and overcome. It's in you. If you believe it, you can achieve it and you can live life at its fullest. Stand up and challenge your challenges. We are all gifted; some just need the courage to open their packages. There is a message in the mess. An English proverb says, "A smooth sea never made a skilled mariner". The difficulties you face are to prepare you for the unseen task ahead; they are to make you resilient, capable and knowledgeable.

We are gods and we carry God. We are not permitted to be victims of natural circumstances when we have a supernatural God. Long and fulfilled life is our birthright in Christ.

Embrace your uniqueness in God. Don't lose yourself trying to blend or do what is in vogue. Don't lose your personality because you want to do what you feel is more accepted by the world standard. God has made you in a way that fits into His plans and purpose for your life. Understand yourself, be yourself because everyone else is taken. Do not compare yourself with others. In the school of life, there are no class mates, everyone is in his or her own class. No same set or same level, we all operate on different levels and timing. Be careful with motivational messages; some of them might push you to do things contrary to what you're made for and make you lose divine timing. If you're not sure of where you are going, a man who has a destination and knows the way will make you go his own direction and use you. A right direction always leads to a great destination.

Celebrate your strength instead of capitalizing on your weakness. People will misunderstand you and make you feel worse but don't lose yourself. Take to corrections but don't lose who you are in trying to adjust to peoples' measures. Everybody can not like or accept you no matter how hard you try, even Jesus who is perfect and with no sins and blemish was hated and rejected. People are going to hate you but you have to keep moving forward and making progress. Success is the best avenge for your haters.

Keep on persevering, the dream land is near. You can do it, yes you can! The Creator has given you the ability. He has deposited in you the power to overcome. It's left for you to discover and utilize that power. God will never put on you more than you can handle. Don't just look at the circumstances around you, look inwards. You were created to solve problems. You either reduce the problems or add to the problems. Whatever you become in life is solely your decision. You have a choice to learn from every situation and get better or become worse due to challenges. One of my greatest teachers, Dr. Akinola Babatunde, said, "Everyone gets tired, everyone feels like giving up at some point; but most importantly, not everyone gives up, not everyone stays tired." Some people defy the odds and still make life worth living. You can be one of those people who doesn't stay tired or give up!

7

UNDERSTAND AND MAXIMIZE THE WAITING TIME

There are so many short term successes today because people don't want to take time to plan and prepare.

When you are great, you don't need to seek for announcement, you will be automatically announced, and even when you do things quietly, the public will know and celebrate you.

God has you in his arms. Feel and enjoy the warmth, love and safety of His embrace.

7

UNDERSTAND AND MAXIMIZE THE WAITING TIME

In today's world, there are so many motivational messages encouraging us to take bold steps. Some don't explain the consequences of taking the steps; a few even go as far as telling us not to mind the consequences. It is becoming increasingly difficult for people to know the right time or possibly wait for the right time to take important steps to their destinies. Not everything is designed to be rushed. Some things require us to wait patiently. Waiting time helps sustainability. Even Jesus waited 30 years to fulfill the main reason he came to the world despite the fact that he has been equipped and informed from heaven. Some of us just jump into things we hear, feel or think about without planning and waiting for proper instructions and guidance. Noah didn't just go ahead to build the ark, he followed specific instructions, he waited and listened to 'how' he should build it not just 'what' he should do. Waiting time is the time to build the right foundation, to learn about and be well prepared for the assignment and its timing.

There are so many short term successes today because people don't want to take time to plan and prepare. Heather Lindsey said, "I learned something very valuable in a silent season and that is that I shouldn't be trying to build something when I was supposed to be cultivating my spirit. I was supposed to use that season to spend time with God, grow, and rest in Him – not step out on faith and try to do something out of His timing." Understanding divine timing is very important, some instructions, directions and even prophecies are for specific seasons and stages in our lives. Wisdom is profitable to direct, let's apply it.

To live a balanced life there is a need to understand the waiting time and setting priorities. If you are a student, your education is very important. Even when you can do other things by the side, your education is primary. For married people, your family is first after your relationship with God. We are meant to take care of our home first. Even Jesus told the disciples that they should preach the gospel first in Jerusalem before going into other parts of the world. Remember charity begins at home.

When stardom comes, you will be overwhelmed that you will miss the days that you could do things without being talked about in the media. The days you could walk quietly on the streets, go to the mall without people rushing to you. So why not take your time to enjoy every moment and make good grades, build a great home or have an excellent career, and set your priorities right. Jesus charged the people not to tell anyone after he has performed miracles, but the more he charged them the more they made a great deal announcing. When you are great, you don't need to seek for announcement, you will be automatically announced, and even when you do things quietly the public will celebrate you.

Take a break, God has you in his arms. Feel and enjoy the warmth, love and safety of His embrace. Don't try to force things on your own, understand divine timing. Don't be too hard on yourself; don't force yourself to tick every line every time, prevent frustration. You listen to some motivational talks, and instead of feeling good about yourself, you feel worse. They tell you to just do it meanwhile it's not that you don't want to do it or go for it. Sometimes we experience situations just peculiar to us and at a particular time all we need to do is to wait.

Waiting time is not idle time or time for laziness but time to cultivate, dig deep, prepare and equip ourselves. To get gold you have to dig deep. Use the waiting time to dig deep and connect more with God. Pastor Busola Adun, while explaining the need to keep trusting God said, "While you are patiently waiting for the Lord to act, thank him, worship him, keep loving him, keep loving people, keep serving and keep praising Him". There is more to building solid foundations, organizations, good marriages than just taking your time. In the days of yore, especially in Africa where I came from, our parents, grandparents got married at young age and their marriages stood the test of time than in the present generation where men and women want to take their time for so many reasons but the divorce rate still increases by the day. This is to let us know that it takes more than taking time to sustain marriages or any great project. Character, capacity, patience, training and hard work are very important. Yes, all these we can have if we take our time to prepare and use the time wisely.

8

DIVINE HELP

Any living thing disconnected from the source is more likely to die.

We have to be connected to our Creator, our Source, and our Maker in order to live a life of fulfillment, because He is the source of life.

The word of God is light to direct you, food to strengthen you and comfort to cheer you.

Worship is a major key that opens, closes and unlocks. When you bow down to God, He lifts you up. It is possible to pray amiss, fast amiss but you can't worship amiss.

*Holy Spirit is a storage that can never be full,
He saves all your thoughts and plans, and he remembers them all.*

When you are tired of everything and you don't feel like talking to anybody, God is ready to hear you out. He can listen to things you can't even explain.

There is no one you can approach easily after constantly hurting them that will embrace you, look over the offences without judging you or making decisions based on your wrongs, except God. God accepts you totally.

*Your concerns concern God!
He doesn't joke with your matters because they matter to Him.*

You don't have to struggle to prove yourself to God. We enjoy the things we enjoy not just because of our faith but because of grace and mercy. Many times our faith is not even enough.

We cannot enjoy life without the sustainer of life or make good use of our gifts without the giver of gifts.

8

DIVINE HELP

"Mark the perfect man, and behold the upright: for the end of that man is peace...the salvation of the righteous is of the LORD: He is their strength in the time of trouble.

And the LORD shall help them, and deliver them: He shall deliver them from the wicked, and save them, because they trust in him." Psalms 37:37-40 KJV

Above all we need God's help. We can't fight every battle with our strength. The Great book made us realize that we do not wrestle against flesh and blood, but against principalities, against powers, against the rulers of the darkness of this age, against spiritual hosts of wickedness in the heavenly places (Ephesians 6:12). Any living thing disconnected from the source is more likely to die. We have to be connected to our creator, our source, and our maker in order to live a life of fulfillment, because He is the source of life.

How can we live our full potential if we don't ask for the way from our creator? There are different ways of connecting with the creator. We can connect through prayer, His written word (the Bible), the spoken word, men of God and so on. In this book, I'll lay emphasis more on prayer, worship and the Bible.

We need to constantly communicate with our maker, and we can do this through prayer. Most times I hear people say let me think about it, I believe it should be: let me ask God about it. It's so sweet to have a good relationship with God. You can relate with him as a teacher, a father and friend. There is a need to redeem the time with prayer because the days are evil.

We also need to study and know the written word of God because everything that has happened in the past, the things that are happening and will happen are in it. The word of God is light to direct you, food to strengthen you and comfort to cheer you. It is a manual from the creator to His creations.

Another important instrument to a life full of testimonies is worship. Worship is a major key that opens, closes and unlocks. When you bow down to God, He lifts you up. It is possible to pray amiss, fast amiss but you can't worship amiss. Always be thankful no matter what. When you hear people's stories you will know you have more than enough reasons to worship and thank God.

God is always ready to help. The doctrines, rules are not just what we can meet up with, we need God. We need the spirit of God. Connect with God yourself; don't rely on other people's faith. In Acts 19:13-15, the vagabond Jews wanted to perform miracles with the Jesus Paul preached and knows not the Jesus they knew. The evil spirit even testified to knowing Paul just like it knows Jesus. When you carry God, even evil spirit honors you. God is the best person to keep your secret. Holy Spirit is a storage that can never be full, He saves all your thoughts and plans and He remembers all.

It's okay to go to people to pray for you and try to seek help from man but in some situations, you have to speak and call God desperately for yourself. You need to stop being comfortable and be desperate for a change, pray your way out. Stop seeing it as usual or normal. Don't take the devil's lie. It's only in God that there is no lie. When you are tired of everything, and you don't feel like talking to anybody, God is ready to hear you out. He can listen to things you can't even explain. Isn't that amazing? In addition, God has solutions to everything. I mean everything! You can talk to man and they won't be able to do much because they are limited but God is unlimited. It doesn't have to make sense; it doesn't have to be understandable or realistic. The supernatural and marvelous God can solve all problems. Your concerns concern God. He doesn't joke with your matters because they matter to Him.

God's love is immeasurable and incomparable. It is even stronger than a mother's love. As humans we are limited but we have an unlimited God. He doesn't forsake us even when we fall or sin just like a mother won't stop breastfeeding a baby just because the baby bit her. God rejoices when a lost sheep comes back to him. You don't need to try to be perfect, just surrender to him and let him help you through. The prodigal son did not try to pretend as if everything was fine, he approached his father just the way he was. Luke 15.20 (NIV) says, "So he got up and went to his father. But while he was still a long way off, his father saw him and was filled with compassion for him; he ran to his son, threw his arms around him and kissed him". Then the father asked the servants to dress him. The father didn't ask him to be cleaned up before hugging the child, 'you don't have to be clean before God accepts you'.

There is no one you can approach easily after constantly hurting them that will embrace you or look over the offences without judging you or making decisions based on your wrongs. God is the only one who forgives our sins and remembers them not. He does not use them to determine His love or relationship with us once we go to him with a repented heart. He won't even keep you at distance to prevent you from hurting Him again like humans do. He accepts you totally.

In Matthew 26:50, Jesus still called Judas friend. The fact that we fall does not stop us from being God's friend or child. Jesus knew Judas was going to betray him but he never stopped loving him, he didn't chase him away. He ate and talked with him together with other disciples. While we are still on earth God will not condemn us. There is always a chance to make things right. Judas had the chance to repent but he only regretted and that didn't help.

Peter stood close by Christ even while fear made him deny Him. He never left the presence of God and that was why he could easily repent and make things right. In Luke 22:54-62, it is seen that though Peter struggled with fear, sin, pressures, bad habits (lies) he never left Jesus, three people came to him at different times. The scripture made us realize that the time difference between the second person and the third man that approached Peter was about an hour. Peter was still there and that was why after the third denial. And after the rooster crowed, the Lord turned, he saw Jesus and remembered. He wept and repented. He did not try to play safe by running away from the scene or by hiding. Running away from God won't solve the guilt. Even when Peter denied Christ, people saw Christ in him. The third man confidently affirmed, saying, "Surely this fellow also was with Him". Live your life in such a way that no matter your mistakes, Christ is still seen in you. Even when you fall, get up and continue with Him. Don't leave His presence.

God is always there, God is real. He can be your good friend and lover. As a mother watching my baby grow, when he sleeps many times he opens his eyes a little or tries to touch to be sure I am around. When he feels I am around, he sleeps back with confidence, and when I am not, he wakes up crying or fussing. If a child wants a mother who is just human to be with him/her every time which is impossible, how much more the confidence we can have in God, who never leaves us. Our God is great, we look up to him all the time and we want him close by. The good thing is that He can be everywhere, every time. He can be with us and still control other things, unlike humans. He doesn't say 'gat to go (g2g) or talk to you later (TTYL)'. As great as our God is, He loves us even as little as we are.

God has not based His love for us on our worthiness but on Jesus' worthiness and based on who He is for He is a loving father. You don't have to struggle to prove yourself to Him. We enjoy the things we enjoy not just because of our faith but because of grace and mercy. Many times, our faith is not even enough. What we enjoy: protection, provision, health etc., are not because we have everything covered in prayers but because God got us covered. We can't pray enough or know how to say it all but God shows us grace, favor and mercy. Some things just don't happen but by the touch of God. Not even our efforts, discipline or even prayer but God's hand.

Yes we need that special touch, the supernatural help. In John 2:10, it is observed that God's ways are just the best. The miraculous wine that didn't even go through the process by which normal wine is made tasted better. As humans, we may try to work and get things done but God's hand gets things done better. How can we enjoy life without the sustainer of life or make good use of our gifts without the giver of gifts?

9

MY LIFE, MY TESTIMONIES

(A personal story)

These all happened because I invited someone greater into my situation and He stepped in majestically to touch me. He turned my life around and made my life full of testimonies. I am Shushan-Eduth!

9

MY LIFE, MY TESTIMONIES
(A personal story)

Childhood was full of joy, pains and hopes. I grew knowing myself based on what people felt I was and the testimonies of people close to me. I was a smart and intelligent child; I loved to ask questions, I was very inquisitive. Like every well brought up child I had so many big dreams and I was doing well academically. The last born of the family and loved by many but there was something missing, something I had to deal with if it will not deal with me later in the future; and that is: Finding Myself! There was a vacuum in my heart, fear of the future and a fragile health. I was known to be very sickly and on many occasions, I had to withdraw to myself.

I remember falling sick and being diagnosed for so many things like fever, typhoid, asthma and pneumonia. It was so bad that everybody around me treated me as a fragile and weak person. They knew me in my school, in the church and neighborhood as a weak child. I was a good customer at the hospital and people who worked at the hospital knew me well. It was usual for them to see me once or many more times in a week. We kept going from hospital to hospital. I knew all the hospitals' card numbers off-hand even as a child. In primary school, some of my mates thought, just as you may be thinking already, that I had sickle-cell anemia, and the surprising thing is that the sickness becomes worse close to the exam period especially promotional examinations. In it all, the good Lord helped me and I always came out in flying colors.

My parents took me from pastors to pastors who prayed for me and many of them said I was going through it all because of my great future. At a point, even my own parents started to think I had sick-cell anemia. That's to show how serious it was. They took me for a blood test and they were scared of the result despite the fact that they knew my genotype is 'AA' from birth. Maybe they felt it was possible for genotype to change because the trials were too much for them. Remember, I had many dreams, many visions, and other visions said concerning me, I kept wondering how they would ever come to pass.

One day I cried and told my mother, 'is it not better for me to just be in coma'? I was less than 13 years at that time. At least if I was in a coma, I won't feel the pain and feel the agony of going through medications and taking painful injections (there was a time I had to take more than 12 injections in a week). She cried, rejected it and prayed for me. She explained the meaning of coma better to me. My primary school classmate who also went to the same secondary school with me told me one day that she thought I was a sickle-cell patient because I missed school and fell sick every time. Everybody treated me as fragile and people were over-protective, preventing me from doing normal things that every child at my age could do. During breaks in school hours I couldn't play with my mates as a child because I was told to avoid inhaling dust or strenuous play. Sometimes I would cry alone in the class. My tears knew no bound. I became more withdrawn and secretive that I stopped telling my parents about my pains or aches just because I was ashamed of being a burden. Thank God they were very observant parents who would call me and ask questions to make sure I was fine. My dad called me one day and told me he loves me and it is his responsibility to take care of me. He said he can never be tired of taking care of me so I should always feel free to talk to him or complain about my health if the need arose. He didn't understand why I will just be crying in my room in pains and pretend everything was fine. It got to that level! I was tired, ashamed and fed up. It felt like I was 'a devourer' of the family finance and peace.

In all of this I kept growing, knowing more of God. I read books, developed myself, discovered myself early and refused to get distracted by peer pressure. I stood uncompromisingly for a worthy course and served God with all my heart and with all sincerity.

I didn't let what I was going through limit me and with God's mercy I kept excelling. One night I had an asthma attack and this time I refused to rush to my parents in their bedroom but I went straight to God. I called upon God, I prayed and delivered myself! Hallelujah! Since then, I started living in the consciousness of my right to good health in Christ and that was it! I never had the attack again and I became whole. I still continued to grow, connected to people older than me even before the age of 15. I read many more books, went for trainings and I was committed to the work of God. I became the envy of many. I remember when I was in my final year in college, out of all my mates in a teenagers' church where I served, no one attended a particular Sunday service except me. We were preparing for our Senior Secondary School Mathematics examinations and we all dreaded the subject. Many of my mates had to stay away from the church. I went and performed my duties. I remember a sister personally prayed for me, she even told me her own kid sister could not come because of the mathematics examination. I was passionate about the work of God. Going to church and serving God was not an excuse for me not to study; it only caused me less sleep and play. And out of all of us who wrote the examination, I was the only one who had credit in Mathematics and English in our two Senior Secondary School Examinations (WAEC and NECO).

I got an admission into the university that same year though I was not given the program of my choice (law). After some encouragements from teachers and those I looked up to I accepted the program and realized the need to be grateful for being part of the few who got admission to a highly sorted school in Nigeria. It was in my third year I discovered that the course is in line with God's plan for me and indeed all things work together for good to them that love God, and to them who are the called according to his purpose. I remember a prayer I always pray: that God should always make me walk and work in the center of His will, that he has all of me and even when I don't understand, he should force me into His will. Humans have limited foresight but God sees the end even from the beginning. I wanted Law based on childish reasons and I would not have graduated, gotten married and completed my masters at the very young age I did if I had studied Law. I would have wasted more years doing what I would later discover wasn't for me.

Now I am healthy, my dreams are coming true beyond my imaginations. I am happily married and blessed with a son; I have an MA degree, more than ten professional certificates from prestigious institutions in USA, Australia, Nigeria and Europe. I am an Author, a blessing to many, a person who now pray for the sick to be healed, a vessel God used to stop someone from committing suicide through care and love, an inspiration to many, all before my 25th birthday.

All these are products of determination, perseverance, positive character, and integrity. They are products of desire to keep growing, to continue to learn and do things that looked boring as a teenager while my mates were having the 'fun of their lives'. And above all, this testimony couldn't have happened without the divine of help of my good God. I remember taking my masters courses while pregnant and the people around kept saying 'wow, you're so strong, how were you able to read, write exams and excel'. And I looked at myself and marveled; the lady who was once a sickly, weak and fragile person is someone they now call strong. These all happened because I invited someone greater into my situation and He stepped in majestically to touch me. He turned my life around and made my life full of testimonies. I am Shushan-Eduth!

This is my testimony, an encouragement to you that when things don't look like it and life doesn't add up, you can always depend on God's love. He's got you graven in the palms of his hand; you are the apple of his eyes where no demon or satanic influence can overcome you. Weeping may last through the night, but joy comes in the morning. Most times the night takes a longer time but morning will surely come. It might look like a longer night but the day will break. And sometimes when things don't happen the way we desire (just like the academic program I got at the university), always remember the end will be good and later make sense.

I deserved nothing but God did more for me. I remember growing up complaining, I was ungrateful. I felt I deserved better. But thank God for His wisdom. I changed my mind because, the fact is, it could have been worse if not for God's touch. Don't be weighed down; don't give the devil a chance to be happy about you. You have every reason to be grateful no matter what, just think deeply and you will discover you have many reasons to be thankful. Be happy, be grateful and continue to do the best you can because you will surely get rewarded someday. In the words of my husband, Dr. Akinola Babatunde, he said, "The things we do today may not be valued today; but a generation who will value them like gold is nearby. Keep doing good."

Conclusion

In this book, lessons that can help live a fulfilled, purposeful and excellent life are presented. MADE TO MAKE IT is written for you. It is timely and will help you live a life full of testimonies.

Reading a book may be an achievement but doing the things written in it and getting better is success. As you have read this book, I encourage you to take action. Don't just read or think. Great people did not get to where they are through thoughts and imaginations alone, they took action! It may start with thoughts, but it doesn't have to end there. Take a step higher, make a move and it will work for you! **Let's work today and get ready for tomorrow, it's not far. Tomorrow is just the next today.**

See you at the topmost top!

Credits

Joel Osteen - Seven steps of Living life at your full potential

Robert H. Schuller - Success is Never Ending, Failure is Never Final

ABOUT THE AUTHOR

Abisola Akinola-Babatunde is a motivational and inspirational teacher. She is God's mouthpiece who has served in various leadership capacities with youths and she strongly believes in raising young people of integrity.

She had her undergraduate studies in History and International Studies at the University of Ilorin, Nigeria. She is a Masters graduate of International Relations from Cyprus International University, TRNC.

She has received extensive trainings from prestigious institutions in Nigeria, Europe, America and Australia. Some of the trainings are: Creative Problem Solving from University of Minnesota-USA; International Leadership and Organizational Behavior from Bocconi University-Italy; Entrepreneurship and Family Business from RMIT University-Australia; Management of Fashion and Luxury Companies from Bocconi University; Foundational

Principles of Teaching English (TESOL) at Arizona State University-USA; Basic Certificate in Leadership at Daystar Leadership Academy (DLA)-Nigeria.

She is a writer, a student of World Video Bible School, an Executive Partner of PATRAL and CAAVAC Global Resources.

She is married to Akinola Babatunde and blessed with a son, Dexstar.